T0145178

Diaries of Jane Summers - Vol 1

A Collection of Letters

JANE SUMMERS

AuthorHouse™
1663 Liberty Drive
Bloomington, IN 47403
www.authorhouse.com
Phone: 833-262-8899

Because of the dynamic nature of the Internet, any web addresses or links contained in this book may have changed since publication and may no longer be valid. The views expressed in this work are solely those of the author and do not necessarily reflect the views of the publisher, and the publisher hereby disclaims any responsibility for them.

Any people depicted in stock imagery provided by Getty Images are models, and such images are being used for illustrative purposes only. Certain stock imagery © Getty Images.

This book is printed on acid-free paper.

ISBN: 978-1-6655-6087-0 (sc)
ISBN: 978-1-6655-6086-3 (e)

Library of Congress Control Number: 2022910233

Print information available on the last page.

Published by AuthorHouse 06/01/2022

authorHOUSE®

Contents

Acknowledgements

This book is dedicated to my father Dr. Chinta Chidananda Rao (Chief Medical Officer, South Central Railway), my mother Chinta Visalakshi, my husband Srinivas Madiraju, my daughter Anika Madiraju, my family and friends.

My sincere appreciation to all my friends, and well-wishers who have helped me at all times.

Diaries of Jane Summers is a 15-chapter book of Jane's letters to her mother, sharing her knowledge of nature, seasons, culture, customs, and traditions.

Diaries of Jane Summers is a way of preserving existing customs, traditions, culture and heritage and adding new differences for new knowledge topics of nature and seasons.

This book includes a short story, lyrics of musical album, Autumn Sacred, and a new piano classic softonue.

Chapter 1

Dear Mother, 12/21/2021

An autumn sunset, a shadow of sunlight, is a color orange, grey and white, a weave of several colors of sunrise and several shapes of autumn homes and trees. Stars, a silver trail, adorns a sky of a night of whispers, a sunset path that fades to darkness, a visitor, rare. A path of several shapes of stars, a star dance a mile, an autumn harvest celebration, I see emerge from the different shapes and sizes, for a cheer of a new day of sunrise, a new day of prayers of fulfillment on a full moon day. A night of clouds, rain, and calm of questions, and answers for new days unknown.

Days of festivities are offered on a full moon day. Prayers of satyanarayana vratam, and food offered for health and prosperity of every for an autumn sacred.

A canvas of several colors and shapes of sunrise and sunset, silver jewels a decor of an art, a weave artsy of a story of a day. My title of the artsy sunset, A farewell of an evening of sunset colors for a new color, peace and harmony.

Love
Jane

Chapter 2

Dear Mother, 12/25/2021

Today I noted the differences in the different seasons over a period of four years and added these differences to add to new literature.

Some notes I gathered are notes that are not apocryphal. There are notes that are congruable and must be written down in a guide for a detail of a note to be passed down to others for lookup of season's differences for a value of a tradition.

A flower, a petal curved for a dress, is an art of a day. A flower several layers for a difference of a flower open, petals that open for a new color of shadows and a pattern. A flower that matches an arrangement of a sunrise and sunset. An ethereal art, a wonder, an art of a match for a custom of a day for prayers, celebrations, for a season such as a marriage, a festival, flowers for a significance of a day of virtues of peace, harmony, appreciation, support, trust and others. A first day of spring or a summer, a difference of a color, I use for a ritual.

These notes will serve as examples for new words we create to extend our knowledge to describe a season such as pensacious, beaugillent, and new customs of hospitality we extend for a new celebration and others in addition to what we know.

Love
Jane

Chapter 3

Dear Mother, 12/25/2021

I noted down the differences in seasons over a period of four years and added them to new literature. Some notes that I gathered are notes that are not apocryphal. There are notes that are congruable and must be written down in a guide for details to be passed down to generations to preserve values of customs and traditions.

A flower, a petal curved as a dress, is a new art of a day. A flower several layers is a difference of petals new, a new color resembling a pattern of a shadow. A new flower, petale matches an arrangement of a sunrise and sunset. An example of an ethereal art is an art of a match of a custom or tradition and is used for celebrations such as marriages or festivals. These flowers are a symbol of art created through sunrise and sunset, and stand for virtues of peace, harmony, appreciation, support, trust and others. A first day of spring or summer, is a difference of a color of art, I use for a ritual.

These notes serve as examples of new words that we create to extend our knowledge, to describe a season, pensacious, beaugillent, steadouscent and others. These words can also be added as extension words to describe new customs and traditions.

Love
Jane

Chapter 4

Dear mother, 12/25/2021

Petals and leaves of a breezy day. A day I need to understand an art of a season to assemble and arrange for a day of autumn festival celebration. To gather petals and leaves, for colors light and dark is an art I use for a pattern, a color and texture, a spring and a summer.

A petal I dress for a tone of a voile, linen, chiffon, crepe and for a color pink, blue, yellow, green and white, a spring and a summer, a purple, yellow, maroon, black, orange and brown for an autumn and a winter. A petal is a coat of a difference I wear an autumn and a winter for a difference of a spring and summer.

Autumn days, are days I plan and celebrate festivals, Dasara and Diwali an October and a November. I offer prayers to goddess Lakshmi and goddess Durga for health, wealth and prosperity. I offer turmeric, kumkum, and sandalwood powder, along with panchamrutam as prasadam.
I light lamps in the evening and read prayers for Navarathri, 9 days of Dasara. I make a sweet dish, all nine days and offer Prasadam to goddess Durga.
Autumn days I study for observation of a task or a family custom and tradition.
I learnt my autumn art during an autumn season. My autumn colors I describe of an autumn classic poem, prose, song, musical note and others.
An autumn is a time I read books, understand a spice, create new art for new knowledge gain in different subjects.

Love
Jane

Chapter 5

Dear Mother 12/25/2021

A spring, an artsy weave of an ivy plant is an art I look at often for a difference of shape and pattern of seasons. A weave green of several colors of an ivy is a difference of a weave of jasmine and bougenvilla for a fragrance, shape, color and pattern.

A spring new leaf and new flower is a new sunrise spring pattern.

A weave of an artsy spring of my kitchen, is a weave I create from the colors of flowers and creepers outside my backyard for a spring art.

Love
Jane

Chapter 6

Dear Mother, 12/25/2021

I see several trees, shapes and sizes during a journey in a train, These trees resemble different people looking at the train, some waving, some leaning to say something, a few with hands up or down for a gesture of something. A journey of trees of a summer view.

I see trees of a winter view showing a profile of a branch with a lineage of a branch and twigs for a difference of a view of a family for an ancestral view. Trees of an autumn, a mix of colors of different leaves display colors of food of autumn such as grapes, squashes, oranges, beetroot and apples red for an autumn and winter.

Love
Jane

Chapter 7

Dear Mother 12/25/2021

I read books for a focus of mind to gain intellectual depth, and knowledge for a use in new studies. I mark an abstract as a note for memories of use.

Autumn leaves is a color I save for an art, and summer colors, a color I use for a summer fresh fragrance of my dress and home.

A winter snow is a snow I await to read a winter book, to treasure memories of a new winter. A spring burst is a first flower, I use as an example of a spring cheer, daffodils, a beauty of color, grace and poise, a feast everyone's eyes.

Love
Jane

Chapter 8

Dear Mother, 12/25/2021

A celebration of a festival, a dance of ladies in groups of eight, a kolatam is a dance using an arrangement of hands, and sticks in two hands to perform a dance of a clap of sticks up and down, for a musical note in a circular motion. Dresses, several colors, with a border gold, and pleats hanging down is an art arranged for an autumn festival art. A natural art is an arrangement of several trees, shapes and sizes, hands extended up and down for a dance in a line, a round, an angle and a half circle. A dance arranged for a purpose of a season is a difference of a natural art of dances of trees. A definition, a purpose, a feature, a season I did not know, until I noticed the difference for an arrangement of an art and other forms of classical dances.

Love
Jane

Chapter 9

Dear Mother, 12/25/2021

Several colors I choose for several arts, and several seasons. A summer art I choose a blue as a background and a layer of icing, for a summer tea party. Flowers I decorate are the white gardenias and a few white primroses for a difference of a vase decor art. These colors are colors to lighten the mood for a cheer and laughter of a summer time. Summer time stories is the theme I gather for a difference of laughter of stories for renewal of friendships. Whispers in groups is only for conversations to understand and know a topic better.

Communication and expertise in topics will decide the leader of the group. A friendship that will end for lack of communication or expertise in topics is a color of a flower that will fade a season, but a color deep is a color perennial that will survive all seasons.

Spring around the corner, Spring afresh, my mind, are expressions to keep spring thoughts afresh such as a spring fragrance for a faint rose perfume, a spring recipe for a new spring note of friendship. Spring reading for a lightness of a step, spring walk to see the first bloom of lilies, roses and others, an art for a learning of new colors of flowers.

Love
Jane

Chapter 10

Dear Mother, 12/25/2021

Flowers I discern a season for a mood or a tone. Flowers as buds closed, flowers with Petals wide open, flowers with petals down, flowers with petals similar a number and size, flowers for colors a difference but similar a shape. All flowers have colors and petals, but a difference is the size, the number of petals, the time and length of stay, seasons.

Several flowers a branch is a support of a tree. A flower left alone is a heavy fall down a branch, unless a group for a support is forthcoming for a comfort, and cheer of another.

A friendship of a group is for an appreciation and comfort of every, and is a quality of a virtue, and a need of all seasons. All differences of qualities of a virtue must be graced for a new difference of virtue, friendly, positive and graceful.

Love
Jane

Chapter 11

Dear Mother. 12/25/2021

Today we went to see Christmas Holidays lights at an island village. There were several cottages around the island. The lights were decorated as a painting of an art. The art consisted of ponies, snow, giraffes, sugar cane candy, carts, reindeer carriages, with prince and princess riding a horse drawn carriage.

We walked a 3/4 mile path of lights on a narrow bridge with the path decorated of lights on either side, reminding me of a winter art bridge walk. The lights had different patterns of art such as a circle, triangle, rectangle, vertical and horizontal.
These notes reminded me of musical pattern of a seasonal art.

The village art at the island can be cherished as an art of family penned for memories of family values, a togetherness of a family memory cherished, a lifetime.

Love
Jane

Chapter 12

Dear Mother, 12/25/2021

I looked at the different flowers of spring and autumn. The petals are thicker, an autumn and lighter a spring. A spring light, is a jacket light and an autumn, an autumn thick that reminded me of an autumn art, a difference of a spring art, light. An autumn festival is a difference of a spring festival, a tulip bloom, a deep violet, an autumn.

Spring is only a path light making way for a summer breeze of laughter, skies bright with pale color flowers and foods for an illness cure of a step light of a spring light dress.

A spring I clean my windows and arrange my summer pots ready for a summer bloom of primroses, daffodils, peonies and roses, a summer dress of flowers, and a summer tea, lemonade, summer cakes white, yellow and pink, lighter of an autumn forest chocolate cake and apple cider.

A spring I am spring ready for a spring clean home, a sparkling white, and a fragrance, a lavender, rose, or a white linen, awaiting the arrival of a new summer season.

Love
Jane

Chapter 13

Dear Mother 12/25/2021

Seasonal changes and seasons help us create an art, a tea art for a balance of health. A cinnamon spice tea or a ginger tea, and a creme bun is an afternoon autumn tea for a family conversation. Several afternoon tea party include honey buns, scones, raspberry cakes, ginger bread and others.

Other types of autumn tea include tea with chocolate or orange flavor, honey and others.

Tea conversations only help us renew friendships or create new friendships for a learning of an art and also for conversing and relating a conversation to a new topic of knowledge. These conversations can be translated to a highlighter or a one line note to create new disquisitions.

Love
Jane

Chapter 14

Dear Mother, 12/25/2021

I looked at a petal of an autumn leaf and a summer leaf. Autumn leaves change color every few weeks until a November, when the tree is empty of leaves. A winter tree sometimes resemble an autumn tree for mildew and moss, and also for a color brown.

Autumn leaves, a color green, turn, a yellow, some a red, some a dark brown until a dry paper brown, to a color that cannot be discerned until dropped to the ground as foliage to blend with dirt,

Autumn leaves are a grace of an autumn season and are appreciated as changes of colors for a transition of a season that one must see for an autumnal change.
Autumn colors are the reason and the season that we lean to a color of food orange, purple, green, and the autumn vegetables, turnips, carrots, squashes and resemble an autumn vegetable ivy trellis in a farm market.

Love
Jane

Chapter 15

Dear Mother, 12/25/2021

A difference of a summer peony and a summer rose is a difference of a peony petal folded inside and a rose petal extended outside. A difference of a dress pleat inside vs outside. A peony dress is a dress worn a summer made of a fabric such as a linen, a crepe, a cotton or an organza. Summer rose colors are the colors that match the color of a peony.

A summer rose embodies a summer grace, a fragrance faint for a summer fresh appearance. A summer peony is a color white or a light pink, a skirt worn with the number of pleats one on top of the other for a social grace. A summer rose is the number of pleats extended out and worn as a social grace for a setting formal.

A summer peony and summer rose is matched to a setting for a conversation, a social dance and a Social grace for a mannerism and etiquette **of** a summer season.

Love
Jane

PART 2

May Summers - A playtime story

I wake up everyday at the same time to be ready for school.
My father helps me put the alarm. I am 5 years old.
My name is May Summers. People call me May.

I have several friends who talk to me, play with me and make me laugh.

I share my lunch with my friends at school.

Today, we have a surprise party for our friend Ann Smith. Ann is moving into our town with her family.

Ann likes to play kho kho with friends.
We played the game after tea time

My friend Pam is bringing tea cakes, raspberry pie, scones, and hot tea. We have a jug of lemonade with glasses ready for after the game

Ann likes to play with cinnamon slides and half moon see saws, a game for 6 year olds. We bought Ann a surprise birthday gift. She loves to play with marbles. A box of polished marbles, a pair of sunglasses, a scarf to wear for the tea party.

I am excited. On the day of Ann's birthday I got up at 7:00 am. The party is at 4:00 pm. We all are dressing in yellow color dress, with a flower patchwork sewn on the dress.

A day of friends birthday. We played a lot and ate the tea cakes and drank lemonade. My father came and picked me up at 7:00 pm

I went to bed at 8:00 pm and dreamt about it in my sleep. The day was the happiest day in my life. I love my friends and my family

A Happy Family

PART 3

Piano Classics : Autumn Sacred

These piano classics are based on the book Autumn Woods, Jane Summers Poetry Collection Vol 3.

Autumn Sacred

A smile I cherish a life time,
An art I remember, seasons!

Grace, seasons,
Days of smiles,
Days of art,
Days of autumn,
Seasons, An autumn, true!

Days of autumn,
Wither a leaf, I see!
Days of autumn
dew, my door, a view!
Days of autumn,
Warmth, a color, a season!
Comfort, a season, an autumn!

A prayer, I remember a lifetime,
A grace, a season, an autumn, true!

Home, a warmth, my tradition!
Togetherness, a harmony, a day,
Days of clouds, an art
Days of autumn, a color!
peace my living, A truth!

Seasons, I remember your smile, every!
A face, a portrait, I cherish, a lifetime!
True seasons,
words, my songs
Songs a carve,
Art, my devotion, an autumn!

Bespoke autumn!
Truth an autumn!
Seasons an autumn!
An autumn, peace, my living, true!

Autumn Promises

Autumn, Autumn,
D# c# d# c#
Promises, an autumn!
A#g#f# d#c#d#
A carve every autumn,
A#g#f# d#c# d#
An art every autumn!
C#d#f#g#A#g#
An autumn, a prayer, a season, I fulfill!
A#g#f#; a#g#f#; a#g#f#;d#c#d#

Autumn, my promises,
C#d#; f#g#a#
Autumn, a new Season,
C#d#, f#g#a#
Autumn a new day
C#d#, f#g#a#

An autumn, a prayer, a season I fulfill!
A#g#f#; a#g#f#; a#g#f#;d#c#d#

Autumn, Autumn,
D# c# d# c#

how far, a season?
A#g#f#d#c#

Autumn, my promises, a few
C#d#; f#g#a#
Autumn, a new Season, a new day
C#d#, f#g#a#
Autumn a new line, a new prayer
C#d#, f#g#a#

My prayers, A sunrise,
C#d#d#; f#g#a#
My beads, a tradition!
C#d#; f#g#a#
my gems, my art!
C#d#; f#g#a#

An autumn,
A season,
A prayer
I fulfill!
A#g#f#; a#g#f#; a#g#f#; c#d#c#

33

An autumn,autumn,
A prayer,
A season,
An autumn, I fulfill
A#g#f#; a#g#f#; a#g#f#; c#d#c#
Autumn my violets,
Autumn, my mums
Autumn, my Roses,
Autumn, a mum, my violet,
Autumn, a mum, my rose,
Autumn a mum, my daisy!
An autumn, a prayer,
I celebrate an autumn!

An autumn Sacred
C#d#; f#g#a#
An autumn A melody
C#d#; f#g#a#
An autumn a tradition
C#d#; f#g#a#

Autumn!
Autumn!
How far?
How farther?
Autumn!
A season!

Autumn Walk

Purple, blue, a color, my autumn!
Green brown, a color, my autumn leaf!
My autumn days,
A# G# AG
My autumn walk,
A# G# AG
a day
a difference, true!
AGFE

Sunrise true!
D# c b
Sunset true!
D# c b
Age, a leaf, an autumn!
Dcbagfedc

An autumn walk, an autumn day,
a grace, a color true!
Sunrise true
Sunset true,
A day of harmony true!

Orange brown, a color my autumn sunrise!
Grey pink, a color, my autumn sunset!

Summers true!
Autumn true!
Awake, a spring, a new Flower!

My autumn breeze,
My autumn walk,
A sunrise, a difference, true!

Sunrise bells
Sunset bells
A day of an autumn blessing!

Orange, red
Purple, red
Orange pink
Orange green
A grace of an autumn season!

Winter song

Winter winter, days of snow
Snow a day I need to clean
Winter winter, days of ice
Frost a day,
I need to clear!

Days of winter,
A cheer, I need to exude!
Days of winter,
A warmth, my winter pepper,
I shake!

A sway to, a breezy day
A petal To a new sunrise
A color to a new harmony!

Winter winter, days of spice, a spice, I need, a warmth
my food!
Winter winter, Days of cold
A soup I need to nurse a cold!
Winter, winter, days of red, my art!
A color an art, I need to wear!

A day To, only to let go of my blues!
A day to, only A day I dress for a cheer, true!

Days of my art of an autumn
Every morning!

Winter, winter, days of art,
A day I need to dress a tree!
Winter, winter, days of bake,
A festive offering, I rejoice!

Oh Winter,
A winter winter
Ah winter
A winter, winter every!
Oh winter
Ah winter!
A winter farewell,
Winter!
For summer I welcome!

Seasons Changes

Seasons you are
Seasons changes, jewels of life
A season I need to know better!

Summers a sunrise, a season true
Summers a sunset, a summer true!
A promise for time!
A prayer an autumn,
Only for days! an autumn!

Seasons a way!
Seasons, changes, a new season!
Seasons, a new prayer, an autumn!

Seasons you are
Seasons changes, jewels of life
A season I know better now!

A grace, a smile, a gift
A gift, A life, a truth!
An autumn, a purple, sacred true!
Seasons a smile,
Seasons a way,
Seasons a new way true!

Saeasons a way
Seasons a change
Seasons a new walk of life!

Seasons you are
Seasons changes, jewels of life
A season I know better now!

Seasons, you are,
Every a season,
Only a grace
A season only better!

Seasons a way
Seasons a change
Seasons a new walk of life!

A bud, a sunrise, now!
A flower a sunset now!

Seasons a way
Seasons a change
Seasons a new walk of life!

Seasons you are
Seasons changes, jewels of life
A season I need to know better!

Seasons a a
Seasons a my my my
Seasons a dream true true true

An ode to Autumn Hills

Hills of autumn
D#d#; fe
A praise of autumn
D#d#d# fe
An ode to an autumn !
D# d# d# fe

Grace a praise of trust and truth!
Bagfg
Days, a season sacred and true!
Bagfg!
Days, an autumn red and yellow!
Bagfeg!

Prayers, an ode to autumn hills!
E;eeeeef!
Tradition, an ode of an autumn temple!
E: eeeeeef!

Autumn, a rock I worship thee!
E;eeeef!
Autumn, a prayer I chant at sunset!
E;eeeef!

Hills of autumn

D# D# fe
My autumn bells, an autumn
D# d# d # d# fee
An autumn sunrise, an autumn!
D# d# d# d# d# d#, edd
An autumn pumpkin an autumn!
D# d# d# d# d# d#, edd

Round and round and round,
My hills,
An autumn,
My sunrise prayers,
A sunrise, an autumn
An autumn
Hills of autumn

Grace, an ode to autumn hills!
E;eeeeef!
Prayers, an ode to an autumn temple!
E: eeeeeef!
Autumn, A flower I bestow every!
E;eeeeef!

Square and square and square
My hills,
An autumn,
Hills of autumn…

Autumn, my autumn prayers an autumn!

Autumn, my autumn flowers
Flowers, an autumn!

Hills of autumn!
D# D# fe
Round and round
My meadows, an autumn!
D#d#d# fe
A Square and square
An art, my cottage!

D# d# d# fe
angle and angle and angle
A grace, my hills!

Hills of autumn
D#d#; fe
A praise of autumn
D#d#d# fe
An ode to an autumn !
D# d# d# fe

PART 4

Piano Classics - Softonue Piano Patterns

Softonue patterns

1. **Steps a pattern**

B5A5B#

G5F5G#

E5F5F#

E5D5E#

C5D5C#

1. **Alternate linear pattern**

F4A4C5E5G5B5D6

G4B4D5F5A5C6E6

1. **Reverse linear Pattern**

B6G6E6C6A5F5D5B4G4E4

A6F6D6B5G5E5C5A4F4

1. **Angular backward pattern**

Line 1

B5 black key F5

G5 Black key D5

C5 Black key A4

Line 2

A5 Black key F5

E5 back key C5

B4 back key G4

1. **Angular forward pattern**

F4 black key A4
B4 black key D5
E5 black key G5
F5 black key A5

G4 black key B4
C5 black key E5
G5 black key B5
C6 black key E6

1. **2 keys together a pattern**

F4G4 black keys together a left A4
B4C5 black keys together a middle D5
C5D5 black keys together D5C5B4 left

1. **Middle keys a pattern linear**

Left F4G4A4 black keys separately C5B4A4G4F4
Middle B5G5A5 black keys separately
B5A5G5F5E5

1. **Black keys alternate**

G6F6 extreme right F6D6E6
D6C6 extreme right D6C6B5A5

1.   Left Two Black keys together and one black key separately

F4G4 together A4 separately

D5C5B4A4G4

Middle two black keys together and one black key separately

B5A5 together B5A5G5F5E5

B4A4 together E4F4G4A4C4B4C5

1.   **Middle three keys together and two keys separately**

B5A5G5 E5D5 C6D6

B4A4G4 C5D5 D6C6

Printed in the United States
by Baker & Taylor Publisher Services